CITIES
PARIS

ABDO
Publishing Company

Joanne Mattern

visit us at
www.abdopublishing.com

Published by ABDO Publishing Company, 4940 Viking Drive, Edina, Minnesota 55435.
Copyright © 2007 by Abdo Consulting Group, Inc. International copyrights reserved in all
countries. No part of this book may be reproduced in any form without written permission from
the publisher. The Checkerboard Library™ is a trademark and logo of ABDO Publishing Company.

Printed in the United States.

Cover Photo: Corbis
Interior Photos: Corbis pp. 1, 5, 9, 11, 13, 15, 16-17, 18, 19, 23, 24, 25, 29; Getty Images pp. 4,
    6-7, 22, 27, 28

Series Coordinator: Megan Murphy
Editors: Megan M. Gunderson, Megan Murphy
Art Direction & Maps: Neil Klinepier

Library of Congress Cataloging-in-Publication Data

Mattern, Joanne, 1963-
    Paris / Joanne Mattern.
        p. cm. -- (Cities)
    Includes index.
    ISBN-10 1-59679-720-7
    ISBN-13 978-1-59679-720-8
      1. Paris (France)--Juvenile literature. I. Title. II. Series: Cities (ABDO Publishing Company)

    DC707.M3847 2006
    944'.361-dc22

                                                                    2005027841

CONTENTS

PARIS

The Notre-Dame de Paris (left) *is the most famous structure on the Île de la Cité.*

Bienvenue a Paris! Welcome to Paris! Paris is the capital of France. It is located in the north-central part of the country. The city is divided into two sides by the Seine River. The river flows westward from Paris to the English Channel.

Paris was founded more than 2,000 years ago on what is known today as the Île de la Cité. The name is French for "Island City." This island is in the middle of the Seine. As

Île Saint-Louis (right) is another island in the Seine. It lies at the eastern tip of the Île de la Cité (upper left). Île Saint-Louis is one of the most fashionable areas in Paris to live.

Paris grew, it spread outward from the island to both sides of the Seine. But to this day, the Île de la Cité remains the heart of Paris.

Paris is known as the City of Light. This is because of its reputation as a center for arts and **culture**. The streets of Paris are filled with historic monuments, cathedrals, and museums. Paris is also an important business center. Millions of people visit this romantic city every year.

PARIS AT A GLANCE

Date of Founding: **250** BC
Population: **2,125,246**
Metro Area: **34 square miles
(88 sq km)**
Average Temperatures:
- **38° Fahrenheit (3 °C)**
in cold season
- **67° Fahrenheit (19 °C)**
in warm season

Annual Rainfall: **24 inches (61 cm)**
Elevation: **315 feet (96 m)**
Landmarks: **The Eiffel Tower,
Notre-Dame de Paris,
The Louvre, Seine River**
Money: **Euro**
Language: **French**

FUN FACTS

King Philip II is called "the Father of Paris" for his contributions to the city. The major accomplishment during his reign was the construction of the Louvre. However, King Philip also had the streets paved and built Paris's first water-supply system.

The Arc de Triomphe and the Arc de Triomphe du Carrousel were both built to celebrate the battlefield successes of Napoléon I. The Arc de Triomphe is located on the Champs-Élysées. The Arc de Triomphe du Carrousel is found near the Louvre.

TIMELINE

250 BC - The Parisii settle on the Île de la Cité. They name their settlement Lutetia.

52 BC - The Romans take over the city.

AD 300 - The city is renamed Paris after its founders.

476 - Paris is captured by the Franks.

987 - Paris becomes the capital of France.

1163 - Construction begins on the Notre-Dame de Paris. The famous cathedral is not completed for 200 years.

1215 - The University of Paris is founded.

1789 - On July 14, the French Revolution begins.

1870 - The Franco-Prussian War begins.

1940 - Germany invades France during World War II. Paris is under German control for almost four years.

1977 - Paris elects its first mayor.

ISLAND VILLAGE

Paris was founded more than 2,000 years ago. Around 250 BC, a **Celtic** tribe called the Parisii built a settlement on an island in the Seine River. The first recorded name of their settlement was *Lutetia*. This is Latin for "Midwater-Dwelling."

In 52 BC, Lutetia fell under the control of the Roman Empire. The Romans ruled the city for several hundred years. In that time, the city grew and spread to the left bank of the Seine. But, some aspects of Parisii society remained. In AD 300, Lutetia was renamed Paris after its founders.

By then, Roman power had begun to weaken in Paris and the surrounding territory. The city was under constant attack by neighboring Germanic tribes. In 476, Paris was captured by the Franks. This marked the end of Roman rule and the founding of France.

In 987, Hugh Capet became king of France. Hugh had been a noble from one of France's great **dynasties**. He made Paris the capital of the country.

The Arc de Triomphe is the most famous example of Roman influence on French art and architecture. Construction on the arch began in 1806, but it was not completed until 1836.

ROMAN INFLUENCE

The Parisii lived in their settlement for about 200 years. They hunted, fished, and farmed. The Parisii also traded with other Celtic tribes to support themselves. In fact, they became quite wealthy. They even made their own gold coins.

Unfortunately, the Parisii's wealth and their island location drew the attention of the Romans. In 52 BC, the Romans attacked the settlement and burned it down. The Parisii abandoned Lutetia, and the Romans took control.

BUILDING PARIS

The **Middle Ages** were a time of improvement for Paris. Many of its now-famous monuments were erected during this period. Workers started construction on the Notre-Dame de Paris in 1163. It took 200 years to build this huge cathedral. And, King Philip II had the Louvre built to protect the city from invaders.

In the 1200s, Paris emerged as a center of learning. Students came from all over Europe to study at its famous schools. The University of Paris was founded in 1215. The Sorbonne opened about 40 years later. By 1300, the Sorbonne had more than 15,000 students.

However, disease and civil unrest soon prevented further development of the city. French monarchs and **feudal** lords struggled constantly for power. England invaded Paris during the **Hundred Years' War**. Around the same time, Paris suffered a series of plagues, including the **Black Death**.

Improvement of Paris resumed during the **Renaissance**. However, there was still a lot of civil unrest. The French kings began **persecuting** people based on their religion. Soon, the monarchs had established complete power over their subjects. Parisians became increasingly unhappy with the government. So, they decided to act.

This statue of Victor Hugo is in the courtyard at the Sorbonne. Hugo is a famous French writer who lived during the 1800s. His book Les Misérables *takes place during the French Revolution.*

VICTOR HUGO
1802 - 1885

CITY OF UNREST

The French Revolution began on July 14, 1789. After the monarchy was overthrown, a post-revolutionary government was established. However, this government was very unstable. Napoléon Bonaparte was able to claim power and name himself as first emperor of France.

Paris saw more violent days after the revolution. The Franco-Prussian War began in 1870. Prussia was part of what is now Germany. That year, Prussia defeated the French army and attacked the capital. Eventually, Paris signed a peace treaty with Prussia.

Paris was bombed during **World War I**. **World War II** brought more destruction. In May 1940, Germany invaded France. A month later, the Germans reached Paris. They controlled the city until 1944.

There was a lot of poverty and instability in France after the war. But over time, Paris regained its position as a **cultural** center. Today, Paris is a beautiful, modern city with many historical ties.

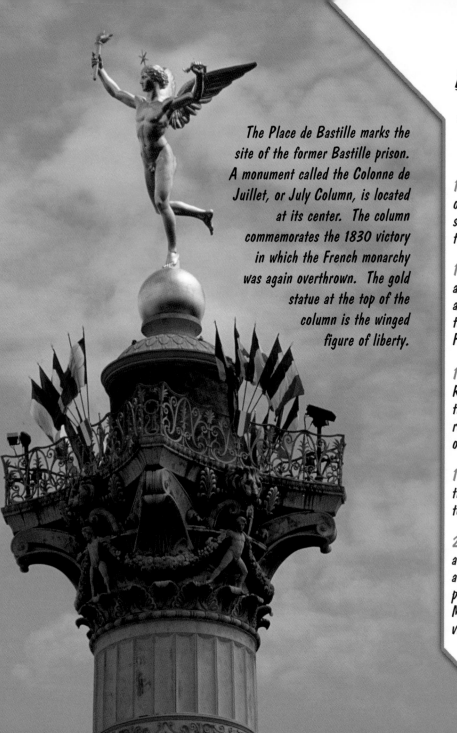

The Place de Bastille marks the site of the former Bastille prison. A monument called the Colonne de Juillet, or July Column, is located at its center. The column commemorates the 1830 victory in which the French monarchy was again overthrown. The gold statue at the top of the column is the winged figure of liberty.

REVOLUTION!

Riots, protests, and revolutions are important markers in Paris's stormy history.

1229 - Students at the University of Paris protested against the school. Several students died, and the university closed for two years.

1789 - On July 14, Parisians attacked the Bastille as a protest against the government. Storming this famous prison triggered the French Revolution.

1830 - Known as the July Revolution, Paris citizens rioted in the streets for three days. The result was the successful overthrow of the monarchy.

1968 - Student demonstrations at the University of Paris threatened to topple the government.

2005 - Two teenagers of Tunisian and Mauritanian descent were accidentally killed while fleeing from police. This sparked anger from the Muslim community, resulting in violence in the streets.

WARD SYSTEM

As a capital city, Paris is home to most of France's government offices. The country is led by an elected president and the French Parliament. The Parliament is split into two houses, the National Assembly and the Senate.

France is divided into 22 regions. Each region is overseen by a prefect appointed by the state. Paris is part of the Île-de-France region. This region consists of the City of Paris and its suburbs. Île-de-France is about 4,640 square miles (12,000 sq km). It is the most populated region in the country.

The City of Paris is its own political unit, or *commune*, within the Île-de-France region. The city is governed by a mayor and a council. The council is elected every six years. The councillors then elect their mayor. Paris's first mayor was elected in 1977. Mayor Bertrand Delanoe was elected in 2001.

Paris is under a ward system of government. This means it is further divided into 20 smaller areas called arrondissements, or wards. Each ward is led by its own mayor and local council.

Hôtel de Ville isn't a hotel at all. It is Paris's city hall! Stretching out in front of city hall is Place de l'Hôtel de Ville. Many protests, celebrations, and public executions have taken place in this square.

GETTING AROUND

Many people say Paris has the best public transportation system of any major world city. The subway, or Métro, is the most commonly used mode of transportation. It has more than 350 stations and carries about 5 million passengers a day! Buses also help the city's people get from place to place.

Paris is the hub of France's highway network. The Boulevard Peripherique makes a circle around the city. This expressway connects Paris to highways that fan out across the country. Rail lines in Paris also connect to the national network.

The Seine River is used for industry and pleasure

The Champs-Élysées is Paris's main thoroughfare.

Many of Paris's wide avenues and new roadways were created to decrease congestion. However, traffic is still a problem on the city's older, narrow streets.

travel. Paris is the largest inland port in France. Barges carrying goods travel westward to the larger ocean port of Le Havre or on to the English Channel. Many people also take riverboat cruises to sightsee. There are 35 bridges to pass under while traveling through Paris on the Seine.

Paris also has two main airports. Charles de Gaulle is the primary international airport. It is named after a French president. Orly Airport is older and is used mainly for domestic and charter flights.

PARIS AT WORK

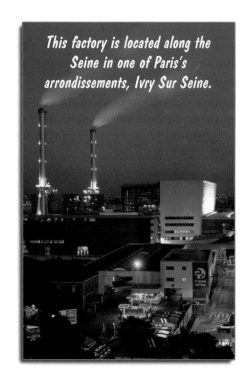

This factory is located along the Seine in one of Paris's arrondissements, Ivry Sur Seine.

Paris is a major financial and commercial center. Many people work in banking, finance, or other private businesses. And as a capital city, about 700,000 people work in government jobs.

One-quarter of France's workforce is employed in manufacturing and engineering. Most of the country's plants and factories are located in its southern regions. However, many large manufacturing firms are headquartered in Paris. This is so their offices are close to major banks and other important businesses.

Some factories are located in Paris's suburbs. These factories make cars, chemicals, and heavy machinery. There are also some smaller factories and workshops near the center

Paris is considered an international fashion capital. Many of the newest and most unusual fashions come out of this trendy city. People come from all over the world to shop at its many fine clothing, jewelry, and perfume stores.

of the city. These shops are devoted mainly to handicrafts and luxury items, such as clothing, jewelry, perfume, and furniture.

Services related to tourism are also an important part of Paris's **economy**. Millions of people travel to Paris every year. They visit the city's museums, shop in its stores, and eat in its restaurants.

NICE WEATHER

Paris is in western Europe. And, it is located fairly close to the Atlantic Ocean. This gives Paris a temperate climate. It is usually not very hot or very cold. The weather is extremely varied, however.

Winter is the wet season in Paris. Heavy rains are common during this time of year. Snow is rare, but not unheard of. However, there are seldom more than 35 days with temperatures below 32 degrees Fahrenheit (0°C) per year. Still, the wind can be especially cold in the winter.

Summers in Paris are hot. The hottest days occur in July and August. So, Parisians often head west or south to the beaches in the summer months.

Fall and spring are typically warm during the day, with cool nights. For this reason, the best months to visit Paris are May and June, or September and October.

RIGHT BANK LEFT BANK

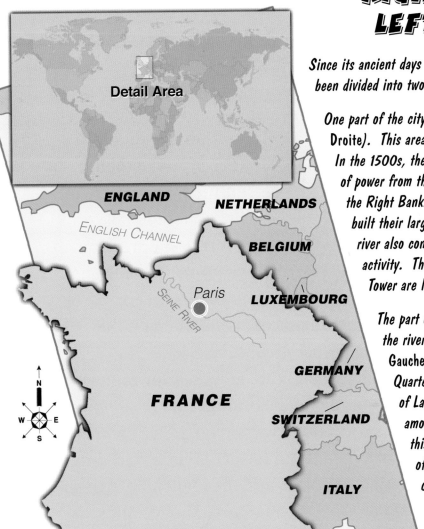

Detail Area

ENGLAND
NETHERLANDS

ENGLISH CHANNEL

BELGIUM

SEINE RIVER
Paris

LUXEMBOURG

GERMANY

FRANCE

SWITZERLAND

ITALY

MEDITERRANEAN SEA

N
W E
S

Since its ancient days as a Roman city, Paris has been divided into two parts by the Seine River.

One part of the city is called the Right Bank (Rive Droite). This area is on the north side of the river. In the 1500s, the French monarchy moved the seat of power from the Île de la Cité to the Louvre on the Right Bank. This is also where Paris's rich built their large homes. Today, this side of the river also contains much of the city's economic activity. The Arc de Triomphe and the Eiffel Tower are located on the Right Bank.

The part of the city on the south side of the river is called the Left Bank (Rive Gauche). It is also known as the Latin Quarter. It got this name from the use of Latin as the common language among Paris's student population. To this day, the Left Bank is the center of art and learning. The University of Paris, which includes the Sorbonne, is located on the Left Bank, as well as many beautiful churches and museums.

PARISIANS

Paris apartment houses

French people are very proud of their **culture**. So, visitors to Paris should make an effort to observe French **customs**. Having good manners is very important. When greeting friends or acquaintances, the French typically kiss each other on both cheeks.

Most people who live in Paris are French. However, Paris-born Parisians are outnumbered by **immigrants** from France's other regions. Paris is home to many foreign immigrants, too. Most immigrants move there from former French colonies, such as Algeria, Morocco, Tunisia, and the French Caribbean.

The majority of Parisians are Roman Catholic. And, Muslim is the second-largest religious group. There is also a flourishing Jewish community in Paris.

A popular family activity is watching the Trocadéro fountains near the Eiffel Tower.

The most common language in Paris is French. Many people also speak English. In fact, French children often learn English in school. Still, Parisians appreciate it when non-French speaking tourists try to speak their language.

French children must attend school until they are at least 16. Children attend primary school, junior secondary school, and then the lycée, or senior secondary school. Most of Paris's schools are overseen by the French government. However,

The Sorbonne

there are also private, nonstate schools that are run by the Catholic Church.

Paris has been an important center for education for most of its history. The University of Paris is the largest university in the city and one of Europe's oldest.

Many colleges are part of the school. The most reputable is the Sorbonne. Paris also has more than 100 grandes écoles, which are similar to community or technical colleges.

More than anything, France is famous for its cuisine. Parisians love food. The centerpieces of the French diet are bread, cheese, and processed meats. Long loaves of bread called baguettes are available at any Parisian bakery. Pâté is a meat paste that is usually spread on bread. And, France has nearly 500 varieties of cheese.

Paris is known for serving some of the finest food in the world! Here, a chef demonstrates cooking techniques to a group of students at one of Paris's renowned culinary schools.

LEISURE TIME

For hundreds of years, Paris has been considered the main **cultural** center of the West. Many people come to Paris to become artists or writers. The Latin Quarter is an entire neighborhood centered around learning and the arts. Most of Paris's theaters, opera houses, and concert halls are located there.

The Louvre is the most famous museum in the world. It was originally constructed as a fortress in the 1200s. Then in 1793, it was turned into a museum. Today, more than 30,000 paintings are on display there. The Louvre contains many important works, including the *Venus de Milo* and the *Mona Lisa*. Other famous museums in Paris include the Musée d'Orsay and Centre Pompidou.

Football, or *le foot*, and rugby are two of the most popular sports in France. Tennis is also very popular. In fact, Paris's biggest sporting event of the year is a tennis tournament called the French Open. And each July, people gather along the Champs-Élysées to watch the final stretch of the Tour de France, an international cycling tournament.

It is also enjoyable just to stroll through the streets of Paris. People can sample the finest Parisian food in sidewalk cafés all over the city. And, many believe that Paris offers a better shopping experience than any other large city.

One of the Louvre's entrances is covered by a glass pyramid designed by Chinese architect I.M. Pei. The pyramid was completed in 1989. Also located near this entrance is a statue of Emperor Napoléon III.

Parisians celebrate Bastille Day by watching fireworks over the Eiffel Tower. Bastille Day is the most important holiday in France. It marks the beginning of the French Revolution.

Paris is full of historic buildings and monuments. The most famous is the Eiffel Tower. This metal tower was built in 1889 for the Paris Exposition. It is 1,063 feet (324 m) tall. At the time that it was built, it was the tallest building in the world. Six million people climb to the top every year.

The Arc de Triomphe is another important monument. Napoléon I had this giant stone archway built to celebrate his victories in battle. It was finished in 1836. The arch is at one end of the Champs-Élysées, the most well-known avenue in Paris.

Paris's many churches are exciting places to visit, too. Many visitors walk through Notre-Dame de

Paris. It is the oldest and largest cathedral in Paris. Others visit Sainte-Chapelle to view its beautiful stained-glass windows. Paris's long history and many attractions make it an exciting place to visit!

Sacred Heart Basilica overlooks Paris from its place at the top of Montmartre Hill. Montmartre is the highest point in the city.

GLOSSARY

Black Death - a deadly disease that spread throughout Europe between 1347 and 1352.

Celt - a member of a tribe of early people that lived throughout Europe and western Asia.

culture - the customs, arts, and tools of a nation or people at a certain time.

custom - a habit of a group that is passed on through generations.

dynasty - a series of rulers who belong to the same family.

economy - the way a nation uses its money, goods, and natural resources.

feudal - a ranked social system, where people had to pay in order to farm the land.

Hundred Years' War - from 1337 to 1453, a series of conflicts between England and France. The central conflict was over who controlled parts of France.

immigrate - to enter another country to live. A person who immigrates is called an immigrant.

Middle Ages - the period of European history from AD 500 to 1500.

persecute - to harass someone because of his or her origin, religion, or other beliefs.

Renaissance - a revival of art and learning that began in Italy during the 1300s.

World War I - from 1914 to 1918, fought in Europe. Great Britain, France, Russia, the United States, and their allies were on one side. Germany, Austria-Hungary, and their allies were on the other side.

World War II - from 1939 to 1945, fought in Europe, Asia, and Africa. Great Britain, France, the United States, the Soviet Union, and their allies were on one side. Germany, Italy, Japan, and their allies were on the other side.

SAYING IT

arrondissement – a-rohn-dee-SMAHN
Celtic – KEHL-tihk
Champs-Élysées – shahn zay-lee-ZAY
grandes écoles – grahn day-KAWLS
Île de la Cité – eel duh law see-TAY
Louvre – LOO-vruh
lycée – lee-SAY
Notre-Dame de Paris – NAW-truh dahm duh pah-REE
pâté – pah-TAY
Seine – SEHN

WEB SITES

To learn more about Paris, visit ABDO Publishing Company on the World Wide Web at **www.abdopublishing.com**. Web sites about Paris are featured on our Book Links page. These links are routinely monitored and updated to provide the most current information available.

INDEX